HAPPINESS ON STEROIDS SERIES

STEP BACK TO LEAP FORWARD

Leveraging Time Off for Maximum Success

STEP BACK TO LEAP FORWARD
Copyright © 2019 by George Zelina

All rights reserved. This book or any portion thereof may not be reproduced or used in any manner whatsoever without the express written permission of the publisher except for the use of brief quotations in a book review.

HAPPINESS ON STEROIDS SERIES

STEP BACK TO LEAP FORWARD

Leveraging Time Off for Maximum Success

GEORGE ZELINA

Table of Contents

Foreword	7
An Overview	12
Getting Ready to Live Your Dreams	16
Month 1 – Doing Nothing	22
Meditation 101	28
Family and Friends – Quality Time	36
Solitude	40
Month 2 – Building Habits	44
The Psychology of Habit Formation	49
Dragon Slayers & Easy Riders	53
Month 3 – Strengthening Willpower	59
Going Through the Motions	65
Learn to Say NO	72
Leaping Ahead	74
Final Thoughts	84

Foreword

This book is for those restless spirits who are brave enough to leave the comfort of their cubicles and start new lives as entrepreneurs. More specifically it's for those who are not only restless but smart to boot. I can tell how smart you are. After all, you're intelligent enough to know that taking a break after leaving your job is an investment that will pay big dividends when you dive back into the fray.

If you're taking some time off to start a new career and want to get the most out of your break and the chapter of your life that follows, this book will be your guide. It will show you how to use your time off to the greatest possible advantage, first to recharge your mental batteries and then to position yourself for future success. With hard work, perseverance, and a solid plan, you can live the life of your dreams. And this book will show you how.

Dare You Ditch the 9 to 5?
In 2008 and at aged just 28; Davy Russell quit his office job. He boxed up his stuff and left – just like that – with the intention of living for himself. Was it madness? Or was it the tangible next step towards living the life that he had always dreamed of? Given that Davy now makes a comfortable living without the need for the 9 to 5 day job – it seems that his decision to leave full-time employment behind turned out for the better.

Similar stories are popping up all over the internet: of people who have packed in full-time jobs and gone off to travel the world using some internet scheme or other. The truth of the matter is that if the 9 to 5 life makes you unhappy, then there are ways you can make money without having to engage in it and finding those revenue streams is what is going to enable you to live your dream.

Can You Live without the 9 to 5?
Working full time for decades is exhausting, making the modern world relentless. We are under a constant barrage of pressure, responsibility and a whole host of other tiny problems that all add up to get us down. I had dreamed for years of pulling the plug on office work one day... of quitting it for the final time and spending three months of pure, quality time with my nearest and dearest.

It may seem like I experienced the life of Riley in those first few days, but I had the same anxieties anyone else would have. One thing I also had was a determination to make my plan a success so that I could go on to adopt a life I wanted to live, instead of spending my best years slaving for a company that would just replace me in a week if I died.

Unfortunately for me, I had spent half of my life working for a company that had a sort of subconscious control over me. I knew all about memos and spreadsheets, for example, but I had forgotten some pretty basic skills in the process. Things like how to relax without worrying about tomorrow, and how to simply 'do' nothing.

There were whole areas of my life that I had lost touch with; hobbies long since forgotten and relatives that I hadn't seen since I was a child. And although these formed some of the reasons that made me went to ditch the 9 to 5 in the first place; they were also a little daunting when I first tried my experiment. After all, I had a whole lot of new time on my schedule and no valid reason to put off visiting Great Aunty June any longer... although I am still not sure if that was a pro or a con.

How to Escape the 9 to 5
There are a number of ways you can go about ridding yourself of the 9 to 5, but the vast majority of them involve being your own boss. If you want to break free of the routine, it will take effort and determination – make no mistake about it. You will have to work hard, but you will be working hard secure in the knowledge that you are doing it for yourself, and not for someone else!

Being Your Own Boss
Full disclosure, folks. I'm the kind of guy who thinks entrepreneurship is the right path for just about everybody. Ok, that's an exaggeration, but only a slight one. I believe entrepreneurship is a cure for many of the ills that plague society. Think about it. With their useful products, life-enhancing innovations, and positive economic impact, entrepreneurs genuinely make the world a better place. What's not to like?

But of course, entrepreneurship isn't for everybody. And there are many other fascinating walks of life. This is a book for anyone who wants to succeed. Whether that means succeeding at entrepreneurship or succeeding while working for someone else, I want you to come out of your break being the best "you" you can be.

As a heads up, there will be times where I address entrepreneurs, seemingly to the exclusion of everyone else. I hope that the non-entrepreneurs reading along don't simply skim over these parts, as I believe they contain kernels of wisdom that are helpful to all.

Start Your Own Side Business
Start your own business in your out-of-office hours. You can continue to build it even as you are taking a regular wage from your normal job. Creating multiple revenue streams is key here, and the more you can make independently – the better!

Suggestions on how to start your own business include finding a product you believe in to sell, providing a service or selling your skills and knowledge.

Selling a Product
Product development is quite a tricky business, but if you are crafty or even gifted in making one particular item, then perhaps it is time to profit in it! Don't sink too much money in while speculating, and this could be an earner for you.

Selling a Service
Selling a service eats into your time a little more than selling a product does, but many people make a professional living this way. If you think you can spare the time outside of your working hours, then this might work well for you.

Selling Your Skills
Ever wanted to start your own online consultancy? Now is your chance! Sell the information you know best and make returns without any initial

investment whatsoever! It's easier than you think, and all you need is a well-placed webpage.

Online Advertising

If you have a propensity towards a particular product and a webpage, then all you need is permission from the product makers to run links to their stock. This is best done through a big advertising firm like Google.

Blogging

You could make money blogging by monetizing your pages. Write about your experience in quitting full-time work and place ads on the page or do some product reviews for some extra cash.

An Overview

My suggestion for the amount of time to take off is three months. Of course, you may end up taking more than that, or less than that, depending on your situation, but three months is the sweet spot. Three months is short enough of a time to justify on a resume (should you have to go that route) and long enough to let you decompress from the 9 to 5 life. Most importantly, it gives you enough time to build habits that will prepare you for your higher calling. And that's the whole point really. The next stage of your life will be where this big recharge pays off.

But no more delay. Let's look at how your three-month break will pan out...

Month 1
Month 1 is simple. Your only priority is to do nothing. Zero. Zilch. Nada. Nichts. Or nothing work-related, I should say. The first month of your break is for whatever pleasurable pursuits happen to come to mind. You can play with your kids, go hiking in a national park, splash around in the pool, or tend to your backyard garden. Do whatever you've dreamed of doing and enjoy yourself to the fullest.

Months 2 and 3
By the end of Month 1, the novelty of doing nothing will start to wear thin. You will have fully decompressed from the job you left and will probably miss the feeling of being productive. Doing nothing for a full month creates a deficit in your mind. You will find yourself craving

structure. Just remember, feeling a little down because you've been inactive is natural. And although it may not seem like it at first, this blah feeling is a blessing in disguise. Because the only way to scratch that itch of dissatisfaction is to roll up your sleeves and set your future in motion. The gnawing desire to be productive is the engine that will power your self-development in the weeks that follow.

Month 2 is the time for you to impose order on the chaos. Starting on Day 1 of Month 2, you are going to develop habits that will strengthen your willpower and shape you into a person who makes things happen. Chief among these habits is meditation, but I'll get to that in a moment.

Month 3 is when you will start to see the positive changes that come from your fortifying habits. By the time you end your retreat on the last day of Month 3, you will be riding a wave of upward momentum.

The Journey
It will not be easy. Expect the first few weeks to be particularly difficult as you go through an adjustment period. Being 'free' will require a new mindset. Indeed, this new mindset is necessary if you are to be a success.

What I have found from my own experience is that the plan in this book works. It is not the only plan, of course, but it is the plan that worked for me. And if you give it an honest effort, it will work for you.

Having the right mindset means that you know success is not an accident. Yes, you could win the lottery, marry rich, or inherit a distant relative's fortune. But is that success? I say no. In my opinion, success that comes without effort has no meaning. If you have the mindset that success is about luck you probably won't get anywhere.

Success comes from having won a hard battle. So let's not delude ourselves into thinking we don't have to work for what we want in life. Success isn't an accident, and it isn't easy. But it is doable. And just knowing that can give you the boost you need.

Break Through the Fear
I realized that I never quit my job sooner because I had been conditioned to think that I needed the job, the boss and the family to support. Once I discovered that all I needed was the ability to rely on myself, my transformation could begin, and my life could change.

After the initial euphoria of handing in my resignation had settled, I faced a sort of fear that I couldn't live up to my plan, that my potential would be only just that: potential that never grew to be anything more. After ten days I had gotten past the initial fears and fallen back into a daily routine that included my family, but that still allowed me to work to my own schedule... and this could be your story, too.

Starting your own revenue streams outside of your 9 to 5 is the perfect way to break free of the system. It might take hard work and a few years before you get to a comfortable place – but think of how worth it your life will be in the end! My advice to anyone considering this is to make a plan and just do it. The key to leaving the old office days behind you is simply to adjust your mindset. Before long, all else will follow.

Success is Imminent

You might have noticed that the type of break I'm prescribing is much more than a just a little breather to stop and smell the roses. It's a deluxe break, a vitamin-fortified break, a spring-loaded break, if you will. It is a way of coiling yourself like a cobra and preparing to strike. The difference is as much about attitude as it is about method, although there is plenty of method here also.

Just remember, your success is imminent. Once you make the firm decision to be successful, the matter of whether you achieve your success today or tomorrow or the day after tomorrow is less relevant than the fact that you WILL achieve it, provided you have the willpower and discipline to see it through.

If you happen to be slightly lacking in the willpower and discipline departments, never fear. The super-deluxe, vitamin-fortified, spring-loaded break that I prescribe is a golden opportunity to improve these crucial qualities. But before we dive into the nitty-gritty details of how to develop yourself for success, let's look at how to cut yourself loose from your 9 to 5…

Getting Ready to Live Your Dreams

I decided that I would ditch my 9 to 5 day job and live completely free of office work for three months. The intention was to spend time with my family – but I had two goals in mind during the first month.

I wanted that first month completely to myself in order to spend time with family, friends and doing the things that I wanted to do but had always put off due to time constraints. I mostly spent it playing video games and writing. After your body realizes that it isn't just on a two-week vacation from work you can start to process through your fears.

I had a lot of fears, mainly that I would fall flat on my face and have to crawl back to my boss and beg for my old job back. Fortunately for me that was not the case. In fact, I believe that the fear was what stopped me from failing since it was the thing that motivated me through some of the hard times ahead.

This unlikely idea – that there is a silver lining to fear is one that will pop up again and again throughout these pages. A subtitle to this book could be "Fear is nothing to fear." I want to drive home the beautiful truth that the fear we experience when we take a calculated risk is entirely natural and even beneficial. Not only should we accept it, but we should also use it, as our anxiousness contains a latent power that will propel us forward, provided we understand it in the right light.

As you make your preparations for the next chapter, remember that you need to keep your options open. Don't just leave your job one day in a rage – have a plan, work towards it and set yourself a deadline. Above all else keep your former employers happy, just in case you need to go back to your old life after all.

Finishing Up Your Old Life
Taking that big first step is never easy, but once you have decided to leave your job, there are a few things you should consider doing.

Never Burn Your Bridges!
Write a resignation letter and hand it, in person, to your boss. Don't just walk out and always serve any notice time predetermined in your contract. A good way to ensure you leave your workplace amicably is to cite personal reasons as your need to resign. Do not bad mouth your company and always make sure that you tell your boss of your intention to leave before you tell anyone else in your workplace.

It is important to keep your options open. Should your plan to work for yourself full-time fall through you should always try and retain the option to go back. Likewise, if you expect a good reference and a trouble-free potential future working life; then you should never burn your bridges and keep your options open.

The Next Steps
Once you have informed your employer of your intentions, it is time to start that momentum rolling. The first thing you need to do is make it clear that you are willing to facilitate your own replacement. Offer to train them and make sure your bosses are aware of your cooperation in this matter. Your willingness to please now is what will make your (and their) transition easier.

Everything in your company will need turning over. Any client lists, any information you keep or any programs you have developed for them. You should have roughly two weeks between the time you hand your notice in and the time you need to leave – although some contracts have longer notice periods, so you should always check your own information to see how much you need to give.

Clients will need to be informed of your decision to leave depending upon your circumstances. A lawyer or attorney, for example, would be expected to notify clients whose cases they were handling about their relocation. It is highly likely that these clients will have new representation, and so they are owed an explanation as to why.

If you want to score extra points with your employers, then you ought to participate in any human resource exit interviews that the firm offers.

Ask your employer for a reference before you leave, this way you will have it in hand and save future jobs from having to get in touch with him/her. Also, remember that you have no obligation to stay any longer than the period specified in your contract. However, if you refuse to work any extra time it may affect your chances of keeping the company happy – so choose wisely!

Now Comes the Fun!
Now that you are fully prepared to make the leap – all that is left to do is to enjoy the fun aspects of your new situation.

Plan a Leaving Party
Plan a leaving party so that you can say a final farewell to all of your colleagues... and then plan an after-party at a local gathering spot with the people you were closest to, just to let them know they are valued.

Say a Proper Goodbye
On your last day, turn up on time and be as professional as you were on the first. When you leave, be sure to exchange information with useful contacts or with colleagues you wish to keep in touch with. Say a professional goodbye with a mass email – just keep it formal.

Here is mine for reference:

Dear Friends & Colleagues,

As many of you may know, this is my last day at the company. For me, it is a bit surreal, because I am filled with both enormous excitement and a sense of wistfulness. As I begin this new chapter I must acknowledge the wealth of experience this company has bestowed upon me. During the ten years I have spent working shoulder to shoulder with each of you, I have learned more things than I would have thought possible. Being part of a world-class team delivering world-class software has been a rare and exhilarating opportunity and it is one for which I will always be grateful. Working in the heart of modern software development, quite frankly, has been the most interesting chapter in my journey thus far. And, finally, witnessing a company grow from 30 to more than 3000 employees has been a demonstration of potential being made manifest that I will never forget. For these life-changing experiences and many others I have each of you to thank.

But the greatest gifts I received from this company are the many friendships I have made. These are friendships from all around the world and from many departments: engineering, product, care, marketing, sales, IT, office, HR, finance, UX, local and global communities and many other teams that I was lucky to work with. I will miss you all.

Now it's time for me to take a little rest and gather my energies for the new challenges I will face, knowing that I am better equipped for whatever may come for having worked at this company.

I wish everyone the best and urge all of you to stay in touch.

My personal email is ...

Best Regards,
George

Get Ready to Start Your New Life!
Once you have emptied your office or cubicle, taken the plant home and retrieved your office mug... Once the boss is happy and you have said your final goodbyes – or once the hangover from the after-party has worn off – then it is time to start processing... and that is exactly what it is.

That first month is your processing time. It is when the magnitude of what you have done hits you, and you realize that you need to start focusing in order to make those ambitions into reality. It is a time for replenishment, but it is also a time of opportunity.

There comes the point when you awaken to the plethora of choices that you have before you... when you start to believe in yourself as the instrument of change in your life. We are societal creatures that are taught from a young age how to conform to the system, and I learned that breaking free of the system and making it on your own is the only way to quench the underlying feeling that something is making you unhappy.

It was the 9 to 5 that was making me unhappy. Making that realization was the turning point of my life and, looking back, I wouldn't have it any other way.

Month 1 – Doing Nothing

After making the big decision to pack in my 9 to 5 day job, as per my own advice, I spent the first month intentionally doing nothing. It might sound like I was just being lazy and having a good old-fashioned lounge around, but the fact of the matter is that after fifteen years of societal conformity I was worn out. I needed to recharge or risk burning out before I had even given my new life a chance.

That first month of doing nothing was vital for me. I did not want to switch from one full-time job to what was effectively a second full-time job without any kind of break in between. When our bodies are idle, our brains are allowed time to process matters – and at those in-between stages, you have a lot to process. After all, you've just left a perfectly well paying job and have a financially uncertain future ahead of you... You are going to need time to take it all in.

The Importance of Laziness
Neuroscientists are increasingly finding links between the body's stillness and the brain's ability to 'soak up' new skills. It seems as though our ability to take time off is directly linked to the speed at which we learn. Frequent rest periods are advised for maximum learning ability...

Think back to high school and preparation for exam time. We were told to study for half hour periods and then take a break. The reason for this was that the human brain has an average attention span of a half hour, and our teachers believed that pushing ourselves beyond that half hour did nothing to further our learning. Schools all over the country have since changed their structure to include more periods in a day, ensuring maximum attention at all times.

Laziness is important, perhaps not as important as the learning of a new skill in between bouts of laziness – but important none the less. Be lazy. Process. Give your brain time to adjust before you throw yourself into your new project.

Unconscious Processing
Unconscious processing is the technical term for the way our brain works while we are not concentrating on a task. What this means is that if you are given forewarning about a task, then you will be more prepared for it – even if you have not worked towards it at all. This is because focusing on menial tasks allows your brain to process the difficult tasks while you work – even if you are not conscious of it happening!

By working in chunks and taking regular breaks, we can increase our unconscious processing time and therefore improve at the skill more rapidly. It is in this way that being too busy can be counterproductive.

Worrying is Nothing to Worry About
The first month of doing nothing is essential so you can decompress from your 9 to 5 and clear your mental palette for the challenges you will set for yourself in Months 2 and 3. Also, taking a hiatus means you can put some space between your current mindset and your old ways of thinking. Thirty straight days of tending to the backyard garden will allow that life-draining rat race feeling to subside, even if that feeling is ultimately replaced by a gnawing sense that you're being unproductive.

I am going to prescribe something slightly counterintuitive here, which is not to hide from the nagging feeling that you need to get off your butt. Let that feeling make you a little bit anxious because that little bit of worry will be the spur in your flank in Months 2 and 3, urging you onward over the dusty plane. The sober knowledge that time is of the essence is a powerful motivator. Yes, too much stress is a bad thing. It can even be lethal. And that is why you need time off to relax. But a little bit of stress following your decompression is a helper in disguise.

Take a Break for Better Sleep
The other great thing about taking time off is that it lets you get your sleep straightened out. If you're a person who has an erratic sleeping pattern – in other words, if you're the kind of person I used to be - this is the ideal time to get that problem rectified. There are other books and articles that tackle this topic more in depth than I do here, and you should refer to them for more information, but to boil it down, taking a break and setting your own routine – which we will cover in a moment - lets you sleep better.

This is especially true when you meditate. I meditate in the morning and at the end of my day. That half an hour of breathing in and out while clearing my mind ushers me into an extremely relaxed state. Half the time I get up from meditating and slide right into bed. And then I sleep like a baby.

Conquering your insomnia during your time off is ideal since you don't have a 9 to 5 the next morning clouding your mind with a whole host of anticipated problems. You can dodge the worry that plagues everybody still stuck in a 9 to 5. If you're tossing and turning, you at least don't have the additional worry of having to get up in a few hours and function in an office environment. This is a real gift because sometimes just knowing that the next day is completely under your control will be the thing that helps you fall asleep.

And if you don't fall asleep immediately, don't worry. Read a book instead. My advice is to make sure it's an actual physical book, rather than an e-book. The light from Kindles and smartphones has been shown to cause an artificial alertness in people who are trying to sleep. Even though the book you're reading now is likely an ebook, if you are reading for the expressed purpose of falling asleep, go ahead and switch off the Kindle and pull an old leather-bound classic off the shelf. And whatever you do, don't get on the computer. That will only rev up your brain and make it even harder to sleep.

So... How do You Do Nothing?
According to psychologists, the ability to do nothing and savor the pleasure of the moment can be learned. So even if, as an adult, you have forgotten how – there is still hope!

How to do nothing is an issue long since considered by the Monks of Tibet. They meditate with the express intention of silencing the part of the brain that tells them what they should or should not be doing. Once you can silence this urge, you are able to truly enjoy the here and now, because this part of the brain is the same part that is always working towards the future or worrying over the past. By silencing it, you are gaining mastery over your own thoughts.

Throughout this book, I maintain that meditation is more than just a way to relax. In my case, meditation was the catalyst for improving my willpower, which resulted not only in a successful break but a successful career to follow. In Months 2 and 3, you will make meditation a daily habit. But for now, you can think of it merely as a way to relax and do nothing.

Turn Off All Your Devices
Disconnecting for a few hours can allow you time to just sit and think. Forgetting that you need to respond to people for a few hours can do wonders for your wellbeing – and for your processing time.

Take a Long Walk
This is a favored tool of artists and writers. While they are out walking in nature they are soaking up ideas and getting ready to begin... there is a reason for the phrase "Part of my process."

There are lots of things you can do to 'turn off.' My personal favourite is to boot up a video game and just disengage with reality for a few hours. Anything that makes you forget about life for a while is beneficial here... and sometimes, the best way to do something while doing nothing important – is to get yourself a hobby.

Finding a Hobby
For me, I found that I might start getting bored of doing nothing all the time for those full few weeks. So, I printed off a list of all of my hobbies and I posted them all over our apartment. Every time I started to feel I had run out of ideas I went back to my list and picked something new.

It is incredibly hard to do nothing after half of your life spent producing for someone else – you are sort of institutionalized in your own way. You need to break out of this pattern. For me, I used my hobbies as a way to do something to give myself a sense of productivity while I was still taking it easy.

Think back to all of the things you used to do when you were young, a teenager, or even in your early twenties. Basically, try to remember the things you used to do before you discovered alcohol... Write them in a list and paste it to your fridge – then follow it. Go build a treehouse or go camping. Visit your local community hub and join a class or take a variety of introductory classes (which are often free) until you find a new hobby that interests you.

Another trick to finding a hobby is simply to join a club or class of people that enjoy similar things as you. So, if you like hiking, find others to hike with and find out what their other hobbies are. You might even tag along. One day you could be hiking a hill and the next you could be base jumping from a mountain – you never know.

One thing this whole experience has taught me, however, is that if you don't take the chance in the first place, then you will never achieve your dreams.

MEDITATION 101

That crucial first month of peace and quiet is truly necessary before you commit yourself completely to a new lifestyle. This necessary processing time is something that is incredibly hard to re-learn after a lifetime of being conditioned for the 9 to 5 lifestyle.

I struggled with this in particular. For me, I had spent so many years just completely dedicated to building that better life for myself – and I only recently realized that I had been going about it in the wrong way. I felt guilty. And consistently fearful about the months ahead. Would I be able to make a living again? Would I ever get another job after walking out on a perfectly good one? Would I be able to make it in the competitive world of professional writing?

In order to keep myself busy and alleviate my fears I had printed off a list of all my hobbies and stuck it all over the apartment. I wanted to ensure I always had something to do. One day I realized that by not slowing down and stopping I wasn't allowing myself the time I needed to process events in my mind and therefore progress easily to the next stage: setting myself up as an entrepreneur. A friend suggested I learn how to meditate, and I agreed out of desperation.

Why Meditation?
Why meditation? I wanted to silence my brain, control my fears, and find some semblance of self-certainty that I was lacking at the time. I needed it to progress – after all, if you can't rely on yourself who can you rely on? However, meditation is a lot better for your health than you would think – it's not just about peace of mind...

- Meditation relieves stress – on the surface, but underneath it also lowers your blood pressure as a direct result of this. So, if you are under orders from the Doctor to get that blood pressure lowered, meditation could be very beneficial for you.
- Long-term practice of meditation physically changes the brain's pain receptors and how the brain interprets pain. Therefore, those with long-term, painful, medical conditions will benefit from its practice to help them manage their pain levels.
- Meditation increases the brain's ability to fall (and stay) asleep and is a wonderful tool for insomniacs.
- Because meditation requires inner mastery of the mind, this increased level of focus ripples throughout your life, and you will notice your ability to concentrate improving.
- Meditation makes you happier by encouraging the brain to release endorphins. A few minutes every day can be enough to change your whole mindset and can bring you back to the present – where past and future worries aren't as prevalent as they once were.

Meditation: How to...

For all those who think meditation is easy – you are sadly mistaken. Proper practice can take years to learn, but that's no reason not to start now!

Meditation was developed in ancient times in order to preserve the 'quiet' parts of the mind. Used by Tibetan monks for centuries; its aim is to create a silent mind by focusing on the body's breathing and nothing else. Tibetans believe that a specific part of the mind causes our fears, and that if we can silence it, then we can truly bring ourselves into the present to enjoy life without concerning ourselves about past or future events.

So how do you do it? Well, for one thing, you don't need special classes. You can do it at home, and you don't need to say "Ommm," as some would have you believe. Meditation is about entering a sort of trance state, and not about vocalization. You can chant "Ommm" if it helps, but you will just appear silly, so make sure you are alone or surrounded by your loved ones only!

Pro Tip: Never chant "Ommm" in a group meditation setting unless specifically invited to do so...

Having said that, the first rule in learning to meditate is not to worry too much that you might be doing it wrong!

Step-by-step

The best time to meditate is first thing in the morning, but any time of the day when you can grab a half hour is better than none. Personally, I like to meditate in the morning and the evening. I think of it as a sort of bracket to my day.

Find yourself a comfortable place to be where you feel safe. Sit or lie down but be careful that you don't get too comfortable and fall asleep!

Now concentrate on your breathing. Breathe deeply and steadily, taking your time with your breaths. If you start to feel dizzy you are performing Yoga breathing and are going too far, so pull it back a little. I found the best way to achieve good breathing was to emulate how I breathe when I am about to fall asleep. Deep and heavy, slow and steady.

Once you have achieved an optimal breathing state, now comes the hard part. To completely empty your mind. This is very difficult but don't stress about it. As mentioned above, it takes years of practice to become a master and to achieve a perfectly empty mind the moment you close your eyes – so try not to be too hard on yourself.

If you feel your thoughts begin to stray and your mind wander, simply bring it back. Focus on your breathing again and think of nothing else. It is difficult but not impossible.

A good tip is to start small. Put aside 5 minutes on your first attempt and set a timer if you want to – as long as it is a silent one. Once you have repeated this process every day of a week you can increase the length of time you are focused for.

When I started meditating, I could only do it for very short periods. I was just too impatient to sit for any prolonged length of time. I would meditate for 3 or 5 minutes. But what I discovered is that this was still enough to get me started on turning meditation into a habit. It was the mere fact that I was taking the time to meditate each day that mattered most. That is the purpose of the baseline habit. It's not how good or how bad you may be doing it. It's the fact that you are setting aside a part of your day, every day, to make it happen. It's that you are committed.

After a while, I was able to expand my meditative state from 5 minutes to 10 minutes, and then from 10 minutes to half an hour and beyond. Most days I meditate for about half an hour. I don't set an alarm. I simply open my eyes when I feel that I've bathed my brain in stillness for long enough to get positive results. Occasionally I meditate for longer, and sometimes I go for less time, but half an hour is generally enough time for me to get the calming feeling I desire. As a rule of thumb, the optimum amount of time to meditate is the amount that gives you maximum results while being something you can regularly commit to.

If you keep this practice going, you will notice marked improvements in your health, your stress levels and even your social interactions as you develop a more people-positive attitude through developing a loving attitude (learned from having to be patient with yourself). Most importantly it will strengthen your willpower, which is a crucial ability in achieving success.

Count Your Way to Stillness
There are several ways to meditate, one of which is to count silently. When I meditate I count to 10, breathing in and out on each count. The numbers become a kind of mantra. I count without thinking about it since counting can be done on autopilot. I find this phenomenon of doing something without having to actively think about it helpful when it comes to stilling my thoughts. If I become aware that I am thinking about a certain thing, I replace the errant thought by returning my focus to the count. In this way I am able to reduce the stream of my thoughts to a trickle and, in certain timeless moments, stop thinking altogether.

From reading books on meditation, I learned that the process of becoming aware of a thought and gently pulling the mind back from thinking, creates neuroplastic changes in the brain, namely in the anterior cingulate cortex, the insula, the temporoparietal junction, and the fronto-limbic network. This repetitive process of becoming aware of a thought and gently brushing it aside is what strengthens self-control. The more you practice pushing away the unimportant thoughts that impede upon your consciousness, the easier it becomes.

Self-compassion
From the mindfulness I've gained from meditation, I have learned to show myself compassion. Believe it not, self-compassion also helps you achieve success. For one thing, it lets you be flexible with yourself and move on quickly in those instances when you let yourself down. For example, when I don't meditate, which happens from time to time, I don't beat myself up over it. Sometimes mitigating circumstances arise, and I have to meditate later than usual, or earlier than usual, or not at all, and that's fine also. Those types of adjustments are easier to make when you have self-compassion, which is especially helpful in this modern era of rapid changes and suddenly intrusive events.

Why does self-compassion help someone become successful? Well, what I learned from being mindful of my own emotions was that my negativity about my lack of success was the very thing that was holding me back. This is an important concept so allow me a paragraph or two to develop it. If you're just skimming along, I asked that you slow down and read this part carefully.

Course Correction

When we let ourselves down, when we procrastinate, when we feel that black cloud of disappointment hovering over our heads, the feeling can paralyze us. It acts like a scorpion sting. I didn't realize this until I started meditating regularly, became mindful, and through the insights I gained from mindfulness I was finally able to see into my thoughts.

Meditation and mindfulness give you the insight to know why you're not doing the things you should be. And the self-compassion you've developed lets you acknowledge your faults without being clouded by self-loathing. Self-compassion is not a way of letting yourself off the hook. It's a way of refocusing. Instead of spending your energy feeling bad, your brain is alerting you to a negative emotion and then using that knowledge as the impetus to change your behavior.

The feeling you should have, and which you will have when you gain mindfulness, is the sense that a course correction is needed. And because you now have the willpower necessary to course correct, it is within your means to do so. You simply acknowledge that something must be done and you do it.

After a few weeks of meditating, you will find that you can steer yourself away from negative thoughts much quicker and with much less effort than before. I cannot overemphasize how powerful this is. It is perhaps the most important benefit of meditation.

Put it into Practice!

The very first day of Month 2, when you've enjoyed yourself thoroughly and are starting to worry about your future, should be the start of your meditation practice. When you are no longer chained to the structures that you have maintained your whole life you are suddenly freed up to become what you have always wanted to be.

For me, meditation was a way to achieve mastery over my thoughts and fears. It is a practice that I have persisted with to this day. I found it helped me in so many ways that, once I started, I didn't want to give it up. My thoughts still stray sometimes, but now I can steer them in a positive direction instead of always automatically going to the worst place first.

There is No Secret Shortcut
Although I extol the benefits of meditation and mindfulness, I don't want to give the reader the impression that I am prescribing it as a sort of magic pill. I don't believe any single habit, belief, protein shake, or book for that matter, can tidy up each and every part of your psyche and turn you into Superman overnight.

Self-development is a journey, and a tough one at that. You must treat each day as the first step in the rest of your journey. It is a journey that requires engagement, dedication, discipline, and drive. There is no secret shortcut. But what I can tell you is this: when you dedicate yourself fully to your journey, it stops being a hardship and becomes a glorious mission.

Family and Friends – Quality Time

When I initially made the decision to move out of full-time work it was based on the fact that I was missing out on so much family life. I wanted to spend as much time with them as I was spending in the office. I wanted to start my own career, sure, but before that, I wanted the chance to create some memories with my loved ones.

Taking that initial few weeks break after I resigned was the ideal opportunity for me to start living the life I wanted to live – and that included being with my wife and child more often. This was something that I'd only experienced on bank holidays!

After the first week or so I began to suspect that my presence was more appreciated than my steady income had ever been. We had to tighten our belts a little, so I started looking into ways to spend that all-important quality time with the kid without having to spend any money.

Why Quality Time is so Important
We human beings are social creatures, able to create our own tribe of people wherever we go. The frequency with which we spend time in social situations is directly related to our happiness level. While spending time with the family reminds us of the reason that we work so hard – spending time with your friends is equally as important.

As we get older, we lose many of the connections that we made in our early lives. As a result of this, it seems we have less and less friends as the years go past. Then comes the dreaded years when the few friends you have managed to retain start to die around you, and you worry when it will be your turn.

The essence of spending quality time with loved ones is this: they (and you) won't be around forever. If you continue to slave away 9 to 5 for someone else, then you have to weigh it up against the time it takes you away from those you care about. When compared you will see that it simply isn't worth it. You could be missing your children grow up for a firm that would simply replace you by next week if you died tomorrow.

So yes, quality time is important. Arguably, it is the most important thing you can do – just ask your children when they are older what they remember most from childhood... I guarantee that their answer will be in the little things like having dinner at the table or walking the dog as a family unit. These are the moments that make life worth it, and what is the point in working yourself to death and never stopping to enjoy them?

Remembering How to Value Family Time
In the olden days, I came home from work exhausted, kicked off my shoes, changed into casual clothes, ate a quick meal, showered and then slept. If I were very lucky, I would find a free hour somewhere at night to spend with a family that hardly ever saw me... a family that was growing up while I wasn't there to witness it.

Leaving the 9 to 5 was my opportunity to leave all of that behind me. Not long after my initial few weeks off, I realized that I had to make the most of that time.

Since I valued quality time almost as highly as I valued 'me' time during that period, I turned back to my lists again. This time I wrote a list of all the (preferably free) things I could do with the family – and it looked something like this:

- Dinner round the table every night. This will give you a chance to listen to everyone's day. If you are very organized, you might even try having breakfast together in the mornings.
- Family board game night – we made this mandatory, and it was great fun... but we don't have teenagers... yet.
- Date night: especially important when you have kids. Get rid of them for one night and spend quality time with your partner.
- TV/Movie night – where we bring the duvets into the living room and pig out on popcorn while watching the kid's favourite movie. Once our daughter was in bed, my wife and I were able to enjoy a movie of our own choosing.
- Walk the kid to kindergarten/pick her up from kindergarten... I found myself turning the kindergarten run into a leisurely stroll that circumnavigated the swing park on the way home. The kids love a good park, and all you need to do is be visible.
- Teach them life skills: this is one that you and your partner can both do together. Teach them how to cook, how to tie their shoelaces, how to play football or how to sweep a floor. They feel great because they think they are helping you, and you feel great because you made them so happy.
- Family camping trips – they are fun, mostly free and they encourage your children to respect and love the great outdoors. You will come home feeling doubly refreshed on account of the calming atmosphere inspired by being out and about in nature!

So, consider what your priorities are. Do you want to miss out on those vital memories by working a 9 to 5, sitting in traffic for two hours, eating, sleeping and not much else? Or would you like to take the leap, ditch the 9 to 5 and start enjoying your family time today?

All I can tell you is that my decision to leave that world behind was the best decision I have ever made... and it could be just as positive for you, too.

Solitude

Much as spending quality time with family and friends was a huge bonus during my first few weeks off – I had to plan and schedule in some time for myself as well. I found the perfect time was in the afternoons when the kid was at kindergarten and the Missus was away for a few hours.

I was able to designate that period of time every day to be on my own. Why? Because I needed process time, I needed planning time; I needed to take care of myself, too.

Solitude – not Loneliness!
When I say solitude, I am referring to the ability to enjoy one's own company. Loneliness is another matter entirely and can lead to isolation and even depression. You don't want to be lonely – you just want to be alone for a while... and there is nothing wrong with that.

But... Why?
Solitude has a number of benefits that will echo into different aspects of your life should you give it a chance. Besides being an excellent way to process your problems, it also allows you time to focus your ambitions.

Being alone lets you find your own voice, helps your relationships and improves your ability to focus. It gives you time to think deeply about situations in your life that you would like to change – and provides the time and space you need in order to be able to learn and grow towards these goals.

Solitude from the digital world is also important. Try having a 'no phones at the dinner table' rule or disconnect regularly from all of your devices.

If you have been practicing your meditation skills, then you will find that being alone is not as much of a chore as it used to be. Meditation is a good way to practice solitude and will also help to sharpen your thoughts and focus rate.

Taking regular alone time has the same effect on the body as taking regular breaks while studying does. Giving yourself time to process information allows you to understand whatever you are learning incrementally as you go. It also makes your mind clearer and your memory better, since you are able to truly digest facts.

Solitude is a good method of learning self-reliance too, so bear that in mind if you ever feel lonely.

Being Alone
Being alone might be difficult for those of you only newly broken free of the 9 to 5 system. Much like doing nothing; you need to re-learn how to be alone. You can do it subtly, without anyone even realizing you are gone for the night... or you can announce to your family that you need some alone time and seclude yourself away in a private space where they (hopefully) won't disturb you.

If you want to re-learn how to spend time alone, then you should think about solitary activities you can take part in to boost your awareness. If you are really struggling, then try some of the suggestions from my list below.

Solitary Activities

Solitary activities are a great way to start loving your own company again, and there are so many ways you can have fun by yourself that you would be amazed. Try some of the suggestions below and find out which ones are right for you!

- Go to a coffee shop – buy yourself an extra sweet, full fat, mocha-toffee-latte and watch the world go past.
- Read. Just sit down somewhere comfortably and read a book or a magazine. Spend time with just you and your thoughts.
- Take up a hobby – while I would recommend group hobbies to begin with, those seeking solitude are more likely to find pleasure from a solo activity. You could perhaps try cycling, swimming or surfing, or any other lone-man sport. You might attend a pottery or painting class, or you might simply turn to painting in your spare time. Nobody is judging you; all hobbies are good ones.
- Take a hot, bubbly bath – light some candles, pour some wine... ahhh. Luxury.
- Go for a drive – because some days driving around the countryside aimlessly is the only thing to do. Especially in good weather.
- Join a gym – people tend to work out alone rather than together, so the gym is the perfect way to have some alone time that doesn't seem suspicious.

Self-reflection

Arguably the best thing about alone time is the opportunities it provides you with for self-reflection and personal growth. Alone time means process time, and you are able to come to terms with emotional and mental problems better when your mind is idle and able to fully ponder instructions.

Ultimately, this self-reflection is what will drive you to become a better person – a better father or a more attentive husband. If you can look at yourself from a stranger's perspective and still see something that you like – then you are on the right path.

It is Worth It

Being alone is something we, as a species, need to factor into the equation. All day, every day, people are making demands of you – so it is only natural that we unplug from time to time. When trying to build your own business, however, it is especially important. You simply must have the process and planning time, or it just won't work.

So, learn how to close that door, learn how to be too busy to see people and learn what it means to be in complete solitude. It is a natural part of the human psyche and is nothing to be scared of. Some of the most successful people in the world are loners, and it doesn't do them any harm...

One thing is for certain: even if you don't enjoy your own company, you will come out of it appreciating your loved ones a whole lot more.

Month 2 – Building Habits

Now that you've decompressed from your previous life of corporate conformity, you can turn your attention to the next stage in your adventure. Here we will work on building the habits that will ready you for your future success.

Structure Equals Success
Research tells us that having a structured approach is the key component to changing one's behavior for the better. With that in mind, the matter of what exact structure you choose is less important than the mere fact that you have a structure. In other words, ANY structure is better than no structure. Take Alcoholics Anonymous for example. AA has been criticized for utilizing methods some consider outdated. Nevertheless, at the end of the day, AA maintains a pretty good success rate. This is because AA offers its members structure.

Structuring your time during Month 2 of your break will not only result in a more enjoyable and less anxiety-ridden time off, but it will also help shape you into a productive person who gets things done. You could reduce the message of this chapter to three words: Structure equals success. That should be your mantra. Make establishing your habits and sticking with them your highest priority for Month 2 and Month 3.

Ok, so what is your structure and how do you stick with it?

Baseline Habits

Here I am going to introduce one of this book's key concepts: the baseline habit. Baseline habits are so called because they form the foundation of the rest of your day. You will no doubt have other things to do as you prepare for your career as an entrepreneur, but those things will be inserted into the slots that exist in your structured day of baseline habits.

To establish your baseline habits, you must do two things.

First, I recommend that you start going to bed at the same time every night, and getting up at the same time every morning. As simple as it sounds, this is a game changer. If you don't already do it, instituting this basic rule will dramatically increase your productivity and give your day solid perimeters.

Second, I strongly recommend that you start meditating. And furthermore, that you meditate at the same time every day. Meditation will be your core baseline habit. Regardless of what time you choose to meditate, the habit will become the structural core of your day. As for me personally, I know that at a certain time every day I am going to meditate and that simple fact gives my day structure. My habit of meditating is the pin that holds the rest of my schedule in place.

The reason I recommend meditation is because it improves willpower, which is the single most useful attribute in achieving success. If by some chance you already meditate every day, then that's great. By all means, keep up the good work. But I will recommend that you commit yourself to another baseline habit that you are not already a master of. Two other activities that serve much the same function are exercise and reading.

Choose a Habit That is New to You
Just in case it isn't evident, your baseline habit should be something that is completely new to you, i.e., an activity that will take a little bit of discipline for you to master. After all, this endeavor is about improving yourself, which requires going past your current limits. Yes, of course, it's fun to bone up on something you're already good at — we all like that feeling of being a pro. But you will need to step out of your comfort zone if you want to strengthen your abilities. And that is what is necessary if you intend to meet your expectations for success. If you're not serious about doing what it takes to be successful, then you should stop reading right now and go back to your dull life of mediocre highs and mundane lows. The choice is yours.

Replacing Bad Habits
Willpower means saying no to any ingrained behaviors that are holding you back and saying yes to habits that will improve your life. There is a time-tested way to do this, and if it isn't yet common knowledge, it certainly should be.

The best way to drop a bad habit is by replacing it with a good one.

This is a maxim worth remembering. It's so simple, it sounds like a cliché. But it should be committed to memory and acted upon. Any bad habit - whether it's smoking, drinking, pornography, drugs, social media addiction, or whatever else - robs you of your chance at success.

Even if you are somehow able to function while nursing an addiction, you could be ten times – or even a hundred times - more successful if you can just get that evil monkey off your back.

Let's say you're currently wrestling with one or more destructive habits. You know better than anyone how this chips away at your soul. You know that the knowledge that you could be farther ahead in life acts as a wet blanket, weighing you down and sapping you of motivation. The question is: how can you push aside this sort of negative thinking and get started on replacing your bad habits with good ones?

Using the Power of Habit to Your Benefit
First, think of your bad habit as an opportunity. I know it sounds funny, but having a bad habit gives you a leg up on habit building. When you have a bad habit, the power of habit is already there. That part of the equation is already in place. Now it's just a matter of turning the power of habit towards something positive. And once you give your positive habit an honest effort, you will start to see payoffs. The payoffs might be small at first, but as you build on them, they will grow and end up changing your life. Before you know it, your destructive habits will be relics of the past.

A Final Word About Sleep
Now that you're in the second month of your break, and are no longer concerned with "doing nothing," you can take a slightly different tact regarding how you get to sleep.

When your alarm goes off tomorrow morning, get up - even if you didn't get enough sleep - and put as much effort into your day as possible.

The harder you work, the more tired you will be at the end of the day. Have a fully-packed and robust day so that by the time you meditate tomorrow night you are ready to collapse. This doesn't mean being an absolute tyrant. I don't want you to make yourself sick. Just use your better judgment and put in a full day's work so when you hit that pillow tomorrow night you fall into a well-earned sleep.

Even if you have a couple of rough days where you feel super groggy, if you keep this up, you will get into an ironclad routine of falling asleep and waking up at the same time every day. And that is a foundational habit that will ensure that not only do you get a good night's sleep, but you will also have a successful life all around.

The Psychology of Habit Formation

As you move from Month 2 to Month 3, you will notice more and more positive changes. Your baseline habit is becoming ingrained. I won't say that ingraining a habit is easy. It's not. And that's a good thing! Because if you really think about it, easy things aren't worth much. If something is easy, you won't learn anything from it. It is when you have to push yourself hard that you actually grow.

Most people hide from effort. But they're doing themselves a profound disservice. Putting forth an effort is a glorious thing. It is robust and vigorous and life-affirming. It's what makes you take air deeper into your lungs when you breathe! By contrast, a life of putting forth minimal effort has the cumulative effect of making the world seem distant and dull. Honest effort adds clarity to life. It makes the act of living more tangible, more real. It imbues your life with purpose.

Pick a Time for Your Core Baseline Habit
Just as you have decided upon a set time to go to bed and a set time to wake up, you should decide on a set time for your core baseline habit, which per my recommendation will be meditation (or exercise or reading, if meditation is already an ingrained habit of yours.) The idea here is that you are giving your day a concrete structure, rebuilding it from the bottom up, and bracketing your free time with activities that require self-discipline.

As author Will Durant, once wisely noted while paraphrasing Aristotle: "You are what you repeatedly do. Excellence, then, is not an act, but a habit."

Think of your habit of meditation (or reading or exercise) as the sun that the rest of your habits orbit around. Make it the center of your re-tooled daily routine.

How Long Does It Take a Habit to Form?
There are plenty of answers to this question floating around. Some people say it takes 90 days. Some people say it takes 21 days. The fact is that there is no universal answer. It varies from person to person and depends on which habit you are trying to form. Here's something that I learned from "The Power of Habit" by Charles Duhigg. As Duhigg explains it, a habit becomes ingrained when it has reached "maximum automaticity."

"Maximum automaticity" is when an activity becomes so second nature that you can do it without thinking. Tying your shoes is one example. Shaving is another. The idea is for your core baseline habit - whether it's meditating, reading, or exercising - to become a seamless part of your life. Every day you practice your habit you are getting closer to making it a part of your life.

Things That Will Help You Ingrain the Habit
First off, remember that the act of making an effort is more important than the quality of the effort itself. The quality of your effort is important, BUT making the effort is the most crucial thing. Let's say for example that you have a lackluster meditation session where you only meditate for 1 minute. As crazy as it sounds, meditating for even as little as 1 minute will still move your habit one tiny step closer to maximum automaticity. When you make an effort to do something, even for a

short amount of time, you are still training yourself to do a specific task at a specific time. You are nailing down the habit. And once you make meditation a habit, you will have thousands of other opportunities to meditate for longer times. Remember that if you ever feel lame for having a short meditation session.

If you are still making the effort to put your butt down on the floor, close your eyes, and breathe in and out, you are moving the habit closer to becoming ingrained. You are one step closer to maximum automaticity.

Breaking Your Routine

If you are reading this and you've broken your routine, don't feel bad about it. Feel excited instead. Breaking your routine is an opportunity for you to strengthen your willpower. Making a misstep and then correcting yourself is what will cement your good habit and mold you into a fighter. It is the "step back to leap forward" mindset manifested in a doable action, doubling your return on investment for the effort involved.

By the end of your three-month break, even with missteps and corrections along the way, your baseline habit will be securely in the groove. If it is not yet at maximum automaticity, it will be soon. Establishing a good habit is like sawing a log. Once you've managed to cut that first deep notch - and you're keeping the saw moving by not giving up - it's only a matter of time until you saw all the way through and make the habit stick.

Getting in the groove for the first time is the toughest part. The first two weeks of starting a habit is the equivalent of sawing through the log's toughest bark. Again, it varies from person to person, and from habit to habit, but by the end of the second week, your habit will be on track to become fully ingrained.

A Structured Day
Use your baseline habit to create a structured day that has set times for your daily routines and open slots for the work that comes up at a moment's notice. This structure keeps you pointed towards your life's goals while giving you enough flexibility to pivot and work on different tasks as they arise.

Let's say you need to research prospective clients. Knowing that you will be waking up at a set time in the morning lets you envision exactly what your day will look like and where the time you spend researching prospective clients will fit in. Knowing that you meditate, exercise, or read at the same time every day, let's say at 2:00 p.m., will let you easily schedule a task in an available time slot for whatever comes up. Maybe you're a graphic artist, and a prospective client needs to see examples of a certain type of design. You can use your open slot in the afternoon to create the new works necessary for a customized portfolio. This is a random example, of course, but you get the idea. Knowing exactly what your day will look like in advance allows you to accurately estimate what you can accomplish in the time slots you have left open.

Dragon Slayers & Easy Riders

I believe in being practical. There is the tinsel-strewn world of our lofty ideals – which are very rarely met, incidentally – and then there's the real world, where things don't always go as we plan. Successful people are hard workers, but more importantly, they don't lie to themselves about how much they can do. Most of them are very aware of the natural ebb and flow of their energy. This is a valuable lesson to be learned. Rather than curse the fact that we aren't superhuman, we should take careful note of our own abilities and limitations, and plan accordingly.

Dragon Slayers
If you're a person whose mind is at its most active in the morning, plan your day around that fact. Schedule the tasks that require the most intense thinking for right after you drink that first cup of morning coffee. The same rule holds true for physical work if that is a part of your day.

I'm a big fan of slaying the dragon. And what that means is that I like tackling the biggest, ugliest task first, and then moving on to the second biggest task, and so on. By "slaying the dragons" the toughest tasks are cleared off your plate early on and the rest of your day is downhill from there. You can't always follow this method, obviously, since some tasks have a preordained sequence, but it's a good rule of thumb when it comes to deciding what to tackle next. When in doubt, be a dragon slayer!

Easy Riders
To the above wisdom, I will add an important caveat, which has saved me from painting myself into a mental corner on many occasions.

If you are in a low energy state of mind, where you just can't seem to get your brain in gear, try doing your smallest task first. I call this being an "easy rider."

Yes, I know this runs counter to my dragon slaying philosophy, but one thing I've learned is to be flexible. When you're feeling lackluster, doing the smallest task first will give you enough momentum to ride the wave and tackle another task after that, and then another one after that. So that you eventually pick up more steam and tackle the one big task that is causing you so much stress. And then at the end of the day, you have still managed to get everything done, even if you did it in a different sequence than on most days.

Being a dragon slayer is the definitely the way to go. But if the dragons are putting up too much of a fight, switch gears and become an easy rider. At the end of the day, the results will be the same. This is just a little tip, from me to you.

Exhalation and Inhalation

For people who want to make a living from some sort of creative pursuit, I suggest paying attention to the daily ebb and flow of your creative energy. That means knowing when you are naturally at your most creative. I think of exercising creativity as the mind's natural exhalation and learning as the mind's natural inhalation. In my case, I mentally exhale in the morning, and mentally inhale at night. Putting it more succinctly, I write in the mornings, pushing my thoughts out into the world, and then in the evenings I read and do research and pull other people's thoughts in. For me, there's a sense of having done the tougher, more effortful, work in the morning that allows me to take a more relaxed approach to learning in the evening. With my mind cleared of all the tasks that require my active creativity, I can turn my attention to reading books and articles. I let my mind inhale, pulling information in, and let the knowledge that I acquire sink into my memory as I sleep at night. And then in the morning, when my brain is recharged, I mentally exhale and push another fresh batch of thoughts out into the world.

Incidentally, my revelation as to how to structure my day to suit my creative peaks and valleys was the product of meditation. It is the sort of insight that I wouldn't have had otherwise. I know I sound like a broken here, but this is a concept I want you to understand!

Exercise and Reading
As I mentioned earlier, I strongly suggest taking up meditation as a core baseline habit. It is THE ideal habit to prepare for success. But I am leaving a loophole for folks who are Tibetan monks, and therefore masters of the form, or people who for whatever reason have a strong aversion to meditation. If you fall into either of those categories, I would suggest taking up either a) exercise, or b) reading, as an alternative.

Exercise and reading each have their own powerful benefits. In addition to keeping you physically fit, exercise is a great way to bolster self-esteem. It also increases energy and drive, especially over the long term. As the weeks go by and you notice positive changes in your physique and abilities you will naturally start to feel better about yourself, which in turn makes you want to do even more positive things. Also, the energy that you exert in exercising is repaid tenfold once the initial fatigue fades. This is yet another example of stepping back to leap forward.

Reading will give you the sheer know-how that is required to do much of what you want to accomplish in life. More than likely, you already have some unread books on your shelf that you've been meaning to get to. I happen to think that books on business and other aspects of self-development are a great place to start if you are considering an entrepreneurial career. Regardless of your path, I recommend reading something that is edifying. Whether it is a sacred book in your belief system, a textbook on a certain science, or a novel that conveys a powerful idea in narrative form, read something that is good for your brain. A gossip magazine or the latest issue of TV Guide will not have the same positive effect. Steer clear of low-quality books and magazines.

The Pomodoro Technique

As I emerged from the deliberate laziness of the first month of my break and started writing and researching, I came across a fascinating technique that I will share here, in the hope that this practice spreads far and wide. It is called the Pomodoro Technique, and it was developed by an Italian fellow named Francesco Cirillo. Cirillo's idea was that work, especially mental work like writing, is more manageable when it is broken into smaller chunks and interspersed with short breaks. From trial and error, Mr. Cirillo determined that the best arrangement was to work for 25 minutes and then take a 5-minute break at the end. Incidentally, this arrangement dovetails with the finding that we have attention spans of roughly half an hour. The built-in break at the end readies the worker for another go round.

The name Cirillo chose for his groundbreaking technique – Pomodoro – comes from the Italian word for "tomato." Apparently, Cirillo would use a tomato-shaped kitchen timer to measure his work periods and breaks. At the end of a set of 4 "pomodoros," or 25-minute breaks, a longer break of 15 to 30 minutes should be taken. Then you go back to the beginning and start all over again.

The beauty of the Pomodoro Technique is that it gives you a sense of the progress you are making. You soon learn how to estimate what you can produce in 25 minutes. The Pomodoro Technique also gives you a proverbial "light at the end of the tunnel" to look forward to. Personally, I am much more productive when I am trying to fill the remaining portion of a 25-minute break than I am when I'm floating in the midst of an 8-hour work shift.

The Pomodoro Technique is starting to gain some followers. As a result, there are several apps and websites out there that you can use to time your work periods. The one I use is called simply "Tomato Timer." Simply hit the "Pomodoro" button, and 25 minutes later a light bell will sound. Another button can be used to time the 5-minute break.

Incidentally, I am writing this as my tomato timer ticks away on a hidden web tab. I see that I have only 8 minutes before my next short break. Let's see if I can squeeze out a few more sentences!

Take 5 Minutes to Breathe
Another special tip that I have is to combine the Pomodoro Technique with mindfulness meditation. The idea is that when your Pomodoro bell goes off, you should take a few deep breaths to re-center. A 5-minute break is not ideal for deep meditation, but it does give you

enough time to breathe in, breathe out, and clear your mind. Use your mindfulness meditation to become more aware of the present moment. From my experience, meditating in the 5-minute break is a much better way to recharge than losing yourself in some random distraction. If you try it a few times, you'll find that 5 minutes of meditation at the end of a 25-minute work period gives you the equanimity and focus necessary to blast through the work blocks that are left in your day.

Month 3 – Strengthening Willpower

Now that you've established your core baseline habits, you can focus on maximizing the benefits of your daily regimen.

Willpower is a Muscle
Willpower is what keeps you on track. It's what keeps you from succumbing to time-wasting distractions or slipping into lethargy. And here's the most beautiful thing about willpower: it can be strengthened, just like a physical muscle. Just knowing this shocking fact - that willpower is a muscle and can be built up by training it - gives you enormous leverage over your self-development and your future success.

Look at it this way. A person's aptitude for success in life can be predicted by two things: 1) their IQ, and 2) their willpower.

The bad news is that your IQ can't be improved upon, at least not by any considerable degree. But the good news, which far outweighs the bad in my opinion, is that willpower can be improved with practice. Just knowing this puts success firmly in your hands.

Willpower can be improved, and your break is the ideal time to improve it. Three months gives you a solid foothold to rewire the behaviors that are holding you back, build better habits, and strengthen your willpower to the degree necessary to become a success. Think about what an opportunity this is. You are being handed an unfinished script about your life and being told that you can write what happens from this day forward. How amazing is that?

Realizing that you have control over your own destiny is a little scary, I know. Responsibility can be daunting at first. But it's also exhilarating and ultimately freeing. Whatever you achieve from this moment on - from the very instant that you read these words - is up to you.

Fear of Success

There is a peculiar phenomenon that can crop up when one embarks upon a regimen of self-improvement. I mention it here so that you can recognize it and then carefully step around it. I call this peculiar phenomenon the "fear of success."

I find that when some people reach the stage where they are really starting to prosper, they suddenly freeze up and stop pushing themselves. They actively resist the positive changes that are moving them closer to their dreams, and they allow themselves to fall back into their old bad habits.

Thrill Junkies

Why do some people work against themselves? There are several reasons. The first, which isn't all that common but still warrants mentioning, is that some people are thrill junkies. As strange as it may sound, they thrive on the anxiety that comes from having to deal with the consequences of bad decisions. If you are this type of person, you will have to decide whether or not you want to keep living your life this way. For some of you, the answer will be yes, and that is your prerogative. If your answer is no, however, and you want to change your life for the better, read on. The information that follows is pertinent to anyone who wants to manifest success in their life.

Comfort-zoners

Unfortunately, the majority of people who self-sabotage aren't thrill junkies, which brings us to the second reason that some people work against their own success. I have found that there are certain people who are afraid of pushing themselves for fear of what they might experience. I affectionately call these people "comfort-zoners." I don't call them this to put them down, but rather to shine a light on their affliction so that they can heal themselves and join the rest of us.

"Comfort-zoners" stick to their comfort zone, which is to say that they find a weird sort of solace in living life to less than its full potential. It's true that these people fear failure, but they fear success even more.

It's almost as if, on some subconscious level, comfort-zoners believe they don't deserve any better. They think they don't deserve success. But they are wrong.

Maybe they're overly self-critical and perceive some moral failing in themselves that they need to do penance for. Maybe there's something about themselves that they don't like. And so they punish themselves by standing in the way of their own happiness.

If you are reading these words, and you recognize yourself in these statements, I want you to take a deep breath and ask yourself: "What have I got to lose by coming out of my comfort zone? What have I got to lose by pushing myself harder?"

It's a serious question, and so I hope you will think about it. What do you actually have to lose?

What if you ignored that groundless guilty feeling in the back of your mind that tells you that you don't deserve a better life? What if you thumbed your nose at the self-defeating voice in your head? Try it as an experiment. Do it just for the heck of it. Let's see how successful you can be. You might be surprised.

Above all else, remember that being successful is up to YOU. The simple knowledge that willpower - the crucial ingredient to success - is already in your possession and only needs to be activated out of the mind-numbing comfort zone. It's like learning that you have the key to a chest of gold. I say "like learning" because knowing that you can develop your willpower and become a success is far more valuable.

Again, this insight - that some of us have self-defeating tendencies and that the antidote to these tendencies is to ask "What have I got to lose?" - It is the sort of revelation that comes from meditating. I might not have had this realization had I not adopted meditation as a habit. The practice of meditation opens brand new doors in your brain. It reveals new avenues, new ways of thinking, and in some cases, new ways of answering old problems. Yes, I know I'm a broken record. But come hell or high water, I'm going to get you to remember this point!

Slow Progress is Still Progress
The mindfulness and increased willpower I experienced during my break weren't apparent from the very start. These abilities developed incrementally over the three months and continue to develop still. It wasn't until after two weeks of a daily meditation practice that I started to see even the tiniest bit of change. But once I noticed this quantum of

progress I was able to nurture it, like a flickering flame that I protected and puffed into life, until it became a raging fire that continues to grow inside me even now. The beauty of your three-month break is that it gives you enough time to ingrain your baseline habit and also to let you see the first signs of its benefits so that you can be convinced to make it a permanent part of your life.

I could feel my willpower improving by degrees and then gradually other aspects of my life began to improve in turn. Meditation affected me like a ripple moving outward, eventually touching all points of my life and then touching those around me. It should also be said that a mindful and insightful person is going to treat others better. It's not that I was a total jerk before I started meditating, but meditation did give me an increased ability to understand other people's point of view. I might not agree with everyone, but now I can hear them out and communicate on a more meaningful level, which of course increases the likelihood of a mutually beneficial compromise. And not to turn everything into a business tactic, but this ability has positive consequences in the business world. This is just one of a hundred reasons meditation is a powerful habit to develop.

Welcoming Adversity

To return to an earlier point and build upon it, the mindfulness I gained from meditation is what made me constantly ask "why not push myself further?" With my increased insightfulness into my own strengths and weaknesses, I started to look at life from different angles. I started to see myself as better equipped, better able to swing at life's curve balls. I started to see life itself as a game that I have a good chance of winning. Every opportunity - business, social, or otherwise - became a chance to improve upon my past performances. Every new challenge became a chance to top my previous accomplishments. I began to welcome adversity, rather than hide from it.

I don't mention this to pat myself on the back, but rather to hammer home the crucial point that this state of mind is a gift that comes from meditation. The important thing is to keep to your routine. Go to bed at the same time every night, and wake up at the same time every morning. And stick to your baseline habit. If meditation is your baseline habit, meditate once a day, even if it's only for a few minutes. The same goes for reading and exercise. Remember, the mere fact that you are doing these activities is more important than how well you do them. The mental and physical effort involved, however minor it may seem, is the thing that cements the habit in your brain.

Going Through the Motions

At some point in your 3-month break, it is likely that you will feel as if you are spinning your wheels. I felt that way myself on several occasions. But I managed to sail through these quagmires by utilizing insights I had gained through meditation. It was as if the universe had planned for those two things to act in tandem. A quandary would arise, and just as I was about to lose hope, an insight would present itself, and I would find my way back out. I am sure that you will be privy to your own epiphanies, tailor fit to solve your own particular problems. Nevertheless, I thought I might share some of my own with the hope they may prove useful.

Going Through the Motions
The phrase "going through the motions" is mostly used in a derogatory sense, insinuating that it is not enough to simply perform a task, but that one must truly give it their all. If you are not 100% engaged, some will say, you might as well go home. I understand this gung ho attitude, and I agree with it most of the time. But it's not always useful, especially when the difference between making progress and staying stuck is the decision to simply get out of bed in the morning.

"Going through the motions," as far as I am concerned, is a good thing. It means you are committed. It means you are willing to do whatever needs to be done, even in those moments when your heart just isn't in it. It means working, even when you're tired and would rather roll over in bed and get more sleep. So don't ever feel bad about "going through the motions." Instead, go through the motions with a sense of duty and a sense of pride. Go through the motions regardless of whether you want to or not, and know that you are a hero for doing so. You will be a better, stronger person for having pushed through the barrier of your own inner inertia.

Missing a Day

A lot of people feel bad if they break their routine. If they miss a day meditating, for example, they might think to themselves "Oh no! I was doing so good! But then I had to go and blow my perfect record. I might as well just give up!"

If you are the type of person who has this reaction, take the following words to heart: missing one day doesn't derail the mission.

You don't slip all the way back down the ladder for missing one, two, or even three or more days of your routine. The thing to watch out for is the defeatist attitude that may crop up when you break your routine. Make no mistake, dear reader, it is this defeatist attitude - and not the actual breaking of the routine - that ends up steering you wrong.

To dispel any shred of defeatism you may feel if you miss a day or two, remember that scientific testing of habit formation tells us that missing one or two days has very little negative effect. So shake off that guilty feeling and jump right back into your routine! You are still on your way to achieving maximum automaticity.

The Secret Benefit of Missing Days in Your Routine

I'll even go a step further and say that it is a good thing to miss a day every now and then.

Missing a day is good because having to "get back on the horse," metaphorically speaking, strengthens your resolve.

When you return to your routine after missing a day or two, you are ingraining your routine even deeper, because you are putting in an extra effort to override the negative voice in your brain that says "I screwed up so what's the use?" That extra effort builds your willpower. When you reject the negative voice in your head and do it anyway, you are powering through your inner resistance. Smashing through this roadblock will make the next roadblock easier to get through. And so on and so on.

Getting Back on the Horse
Shaking off the feeling of defeat and getting back on the horse will give you a different relationship with yourself and a better understanding of your limitations. You will know that you have the kind of self-control it takes to become a success. You will know that you can overcome your inner resistance. Just remember that every time you break your routine, you have to get back on the horse. Every time!

Experiencing a tough moment where you feel bad about not doing something and then still finding the gumption to get back to work is an act that vulcanizes your commitment to success. You are in essence mastering the art of believing in yourself. You are starting to understand that shirking your responsibilities will only give rise to negative feelings and drain away your self-esteem. And remember, even thinking too much about getting back on the horse is a distraction. Just do it. Getting back on the horse is not something that needs to be done elegantly. It doesn't need to be done with grace or panache. It just needs to be done.

Dropping the Eggs

At the risk of trying the reader's patience, I hope you will let me share yet another insight that I've gained. I call this one "dropping the eggs." After I established my habit of meditating and was beginning to feel the benefits of mindfulness, I had a rather unpleasant experience. I had just finished doing some strenuous exercises, and my hands couldn't grip with as much strength as they could normally. For some reason, I decided at that moment to take a brand new carton of eggs out of the refrigerator. I only needed to move the eggs two or three feet to the kitchen counter, but even that simple act proved too difficult. My grip-deficient hand trembled, and I dropped the carton. It opened midway in its fall and released twelve eggs into the air. The eggs all broke open as they crashed to the floor. Not only had I lost a brand new carton of eggs, which I had been looking forward to eating, but I now had a giant mess to clean up.

Now typically, this is the kind of thing that would make me angry at the world. But at that moment I had a very different response. Instead of huffing and puffing and getting angry at my own stupidity, I took a deep breath and let the air back out in a hearty exhale. I almost felt like chuckling. I felt as if I was watching myself from above and could see the humor in the situation. Where I normally would have gotten angry, I now realized that the cost of the eggs and the ten minutes it would take to clean up the mess was far from a tragedy. There was no reason for me to feel the least bit bad about something so minor. If I don't get to eat eggs today, I said to myself, so what? Is that such a terrible thing?

I'll buy more eggs and eat them tomorrow. I'll probably eat eggs another thousand times in my life. What difference does it make if I miss out on eating them this one time?

These were the thoughts I had as I looked down at the puddle of yolk slowly oozing towards my sneakers. I was able to put it in perspective. The point here is not about how to perceive a carton of dropped eggs per se. The point is that my regimen of self-improvement was working. My behavior had changed for the better.

Maybe you're already at the stage where you can drop a carton of eggs and not feel any frustration. Maybe you already have the ability to detach yourself from a situation as it occurs. If so, the mindfulness you gain from meditation will give you an even greater sense of equanimity. When you return to the world of work, either as an entrepreneur or an ace employee, you will be as cool as a cucumber, no matter what kind of chaos swirls around you.

Tibetan Monks
Some studies show that the heart rates of meditating Tibetan monks stay unaffected even when a gun is fired at close range. Can you imagine having that kind of detachment, that kind of emotional restraint, that kind of willpower? It's humbling to contemplate. If that example is the high water mark of maintaining equilibrium under pressure then surely the rest of us still have some room for improvement.

But being able to control my anger was not the only insight mindfulness gave to me as I looked down at the broken eggs. In addition to being able to keep my cool when I normally would have blown my top,

I had the stunning revelation that every setback in life is merely a case of dropping the eggs. And every setback is best handled by taking a deep breath and detaching yourself from the situation.

And to hammer home a point that I've made before, but which cannot be stressed enough, every setback presents an opportunity. The opportunity is not only to detach from our frantic emotions but to calmly and resolutely get back on the horse. It is the mental toughness we demonstrate when getting back on the horse that makes us stronger. The more often we have setbacks, the more opportunities we have to practice this crucial craft. And the better we will be because of it.

Why Not?
One thing I've noticed after making meditation my core baseline habit and having my willpower increase as a result, is that when I get to a point where I don't feel like working any longer, I ask myself "Why not? Why can't I work just a little bit more? What would happen if I pushed myself just a little bit further?"

To have these kinds of questions in my head was a completely new sensation. The simple question of "Why don't I push myself a little further?" - and my dissatisfaction with the answers I would typically give - would be alien to my pre-meditation mindset. Instead of trying to squirm out of meeting my own expectations, I decided to answer the question by saying "Let's find out!"

This paradigmatic shift allowed me to work for a little bit longer. When I got to another dip in my energy level and again felt like quitting, I asked myself the same question. In doing this, I managed to squeeze out a few more work sessions.

I wasn't a tyrant, mind you. It's important that I make that distinction. I didn't push myself to the point of fatigue. To be specific, I pushed myself to a point where I felt just a little more accomplished than I would normally feel. It was a point where I thought to myself: "Yes, now I can feel satisfied with what I've done." That's a good place to stop because working to the point of burnout is as much of a vice as giving up too soon.

That I had started asking the question "Why not work a little bit more?" and had started answering it by doing just that is evidence of my changed behavior. It was a heartening demonstration of my increased willpower.

LEARN TO SAY NO

So, before I decided to start my break from the 9 to 5 work, I was a fairly high flying leader. The company I worked for was a rapidly growing tech firm, and the majority of my colleagues simply could not believe what I had chosen to do. They thought it was madness and - being the good souls that they were - a number of them contacted me after I had left to try and offer me work or new jobs.

Needless to say, this was not what I wanted. I quit that lifestyle for a reason, and I certainly didn't want to be dragged back into it, even over the best of intentions. Some of these requests and offers were worth big-time cash – and it was sometimes hard to refuse them. However, I persevered. I wanted to be in charge of my own time, to relax and not feel the constant pressure. My friends and colleagues attempted to bring me back into the fold because they were worried about my life choices.

They shouldn't have been. Much as I appreciate the concern, it is my life to live.

And so, it came to be that one of the first things I learned was how to just say "No." No – I won't drive thirty miles to restart your laptop... or no – I won't take this job you want me to apply for. I started saying no – and people were offended! But I stuck to my guns. I had decided to live my life my way, and there was no going back...

The Importance of Saying "No"
You MUST learn to say no. Saying yes to everyone's demands is unrealistic and, frankly, unfeasible. You cannot be in three places at once, and

you are not obligated to commit yourself to anything that you ultimately don't want to do. Besides anything else, I had a goal in mind. And if I had agreed to all those job offers, and time requests I would never have had time to start planning my new life as an entrepreneur.

Tips

- Know your priorities – this is the key to saying no to tasks that are trivial to you. When you have a clearly defined goal in mind of where you want to be in a few months; you can't let anyone dissuade you from it. Stick to your guns and improve your own productivity through lack of commitment to other people's projects.
- Explain why you are saying no and the people you are disagreeing with will be forced to comply or give you a better deal.
- Be firm – and don't take no for an answer, after all, that is what they are trying on you!
- "I'll get back to you…" - remember this phrase and master it. It is a great way to defer your "no" until a little later when you have properly thought things through.

Whatever your reasons, you have the right to say no. Remember that right and use it if you have to. This is your life, and you are building your dream – and if they are not going to help you achieve it, why let them steal your valuable time?

LEAPING AHEAD

Ten months had passed since I decided to take my 'break' from full-time work. I'd had the holiday of my life and spent all my time doing what I wanted, with whom I wanted. I knew from when I first decided to leave the 9 to 5 that my move was permanent, but for others, it might not be quite so straightforward.

There came a point where I knew I was faced with two options. I could fall back on my old ways and return to how things had been before – or I could leap ahead. I could trust in my own abilities and branch out on my own. What was the alternative? After all, you will never know whether or not you can do something until you actually try it.

What is 'Leaping ahead'?
The definition of "leaping ahead" is going to vary from person to person. To one person, 'leaping ahead' means making enough money for him or her to retire. To another, it means starting a new company. To still another, it means finding a job that leaves them enough time to pursue a creative path on the side.

But with all the different definitions of "leaping ahead," there is one commonality that they all share, which is the necessity of having a plan.

You need to have a Plan A, and you need to have a Plan B. For that matter, having a Plan C isn't such a bad idea. I find that the ability to know when Plan A is not working and Plan B needs to be put into action is the mark of a successful man or woman. Whether or not you have that ability comes down to how well you develop your willpower.

The ability to act decisively is a matter of self-discipline. It requires mental strength to ignore the buzzing chatter of nagging what-ifs that can plague you, as well as the perpetual temptation that we all occasionally have to simply do nothing.

This ability to act decisively can be enhanced. It can be enlarged upon and cultivated, and the perfect time to do this is during your break. By the end of your break, you are going to be a different person. Not entirely different, of course. You will still have the same personality. You will still look the same. But what will be different is that an inner toughness will have taken root inside of you. An inner drive will be present that wasn't there before. Or if you had an inner drive before, it will be even more powerful and more useful now that you've developed it. And this is crucial if you truly want to taste success.

Are You an Entrepreneur?
To be frank, I didn't know for certain that I was cut out to be an entrepreneur until I gave it a shot. I don't suppose anybody really knows until they make the concerted effort. And again I will concede that entrepreneurship isn't for everyone. Different people are suited for different paths.

You might be a person who's on the fence as to whether or not you'd like to be an entrepreneur. To get an idea of whether you're cut out for this particular path, it helps to look within. If you enjoy the challenge of having to think on your feet, if you enjoy thinking about business in general and your area of business specifically, then entrepreneurship is a natural fit. If you don't enjoy those things, you might want to consider something else.

And perhaps the most important question is this: Are you the kind of person who can be hyper-focused and even obsessive about what you do?

Being an entrepreneur means making your business your all-consuming obsession. It means taking responsibility for every aspect of your business and making tough decisions. It means doing whatever has to be done, at any given time, even when you're not in the mood to do it. Even when you would rather roll over in your bed and go back to sleep.

But if you crave the feeling of being in control of your own destiny, of never again having to punch a time clock, or laugh at a boss's bad jokes, then I strongly suggest becoming an entrepreneur.

If your first venture isn't a success, the next one will be, or the one after that, or the one after that. With a system of good habits in place and your willpower built to its full potential, success will happen. If you keep striving towards your goal, you will eventually get there.

What if You're Not an Entrepreneur?

Of course, you might be someone who genuinely enjoys working for someone else. There are a lot of team players out there and thank goodness because the world needs employees who take satisfaction in doing their jobs well. If you are that type of person, then your next step is going to be finding a job that fulfills you. Incidentally, you will discover that job searching is much like being in business for yourself because you are the person who has to get up each day and actively look for your new job.

There are many books and websites that show you how to do this, and I will leave it to these more authoritative sources to serve as your guide. Additionally, if you need a 'bigger picture' perspective, there are many books and websites that can help you determine what your life's calling really is. One classic in this field that I recommend is "What Color is Your Parachute?" But of course, there are many others.

Should You Go Back to Work?
Making that choice is entirely your decision. If you can face going back to work, then by all means do. If you choose to return to your old job you should be able to – if you followed my steps and resigned in the best possible light... If your old job won't take you back, then consider the fact that you didn't like it much in the first place and find something better.

Finding Work with a Gap in Your CV
Provided the gap in your CV is short it really shouldn't affect you. You can tell any interviewer that you took time off for personal reasons – just be sure to show them that you still have your finger on the pulse.

Follow the usual rules: update your CV and start sending it out. Call contacts and follow leads and soon you will be back to normal.

Moving Forward without the 9 to 5

I decided that there was no way on Earth I was returning to my cubicle. So, with that in mind, I needed to get to the planning. How do you plan the rest of your life?

First, you need goals – but not just any goals – SMART goals. That is S-M-A-R-T: Specific, Measurable, Attainable and Relevant goals, with a Time for you to complete them by. Once you have a clearly defined set of goals all of your dreams soon become achievable.

Once you have clearly and literally decided on your goals it is time to make a plan.

The Roadmap

A life roadmap is a set of guidelines you write for yourself that will allow you to work towards your goals on a day to day basis. I do this by creating immediate goals, intermediate goals, and long-term goals. If you want to make things easier for yourself, then work out SMART goals for each time period...

For example: if one of my long-term goals is to be travel writing from South Africa by this time next year; my intermediate goal might be to have saved a certain amount of money while my immediate goal might be to book a flight before the prices went up, or to book the time off work to enable me to go...

You get the idea. You write a roadmap, and you stick to it, and one day your out-of-reach goals might just be easily achievable.

The Business Plan

The next logical step for me was to write a business plan. They are reasonably complicated documents that outline all of the aspects of your business, thereby enabling you to go to investors and present your idea. Investors won't get behind a business plan they don't believe in, so I knew it had to be good.

I have compiled all my tips for business plan writing here in the hope that it makes it easier on anyone following in my footsteps.

- Your business plan should include a title page, a summary of your business, a management or operations plan, write about your market and give as detailed projections as possible for the first year or two. You need to include your financial plans and any supporting documentation you are likely to need.
- Research your market well – the people you are pitching to probably know it inside out, and you don't want to appear unprofessional by making mistakes.
- Get some help from local services – don't try to write your plan alone! There are people out there who specialize in this type of thing, and usually, business education from your local governing body is free.
- Take your time – work on one section at once.
- Review the hell out of it – it's never correct, and there will always be one stubborn spelling mistake somewhere…
- Make sure to mark your figures as "expected figures" and not actual ones. Since you are in your first year, you can only guess at what your actual earnings will be. Be clear about this to avoid problems later on.

How Rich People Think

I'm by no means the first to say this, but it warrants being stated again. The difference between how rich people think and poor people think has nothing to do with the amount of effort they put forth and everything to do with where they put their focus. Instead of spending their time working hard for a boss who may or may not care for them, rich people focus their efforts on increasing their knowledge of whatever field they wish to master and on developing new skills to make them competitive. Designate the areas in your field that you need to bone up on, and make a plan to learn everything you can about them, fitting these self-guided explorations into your schedule's open time slots.

Four Areas of Knowledge That Successful People Understand

There are four areas of knowledge that anyone who is serious about success should be acquainted with.

First, you should develop the ability to read numbers. Being able to look at stats and understand what they mean gives you an enormous advantage in just about any field.

Second, you should understand investing. Knowing a little bit about the stock market is an enormous asset. Add to this the emerging field of cryptocurrencies. As I write this, Bitcoin is changing the world of banking. Learning about cryptocurrencies and blockchain technology is time well spent, as these things most likely represent the future of money.

Third, you should understand the science of supply and demand. It is hard to over-exaggerate how important this is. If you are an entrepreneur, you do not want to waste a lot of time, money, and effort creating something that nobody has a need or desire for. The people I know who have made the most money, and who have made the most impact, are people who are good at identifying markets that are currently being underserved. They can spy a niche and slide into it quickly to provide a product that meets a certain need. In other words, they create something that people are willing to pay for.

And finally, it pays to understand the law, especially as it pertains to money and to taxes in whatever country you happen to live in.

Understanding Money Management
It goes without saying that money management is a keystone area of knowledge, not just for business people and entrepreneurs, but for anyone who wants freedom and security in their life.

I'm certainly not the first to say it, but I believe Money Management should be a required subject in the schools of any civilized society. Failing to teach citizens the basics of a subject that has an enormous impact on their lives goes beyond being just a giant mistake and hints at a sort of tyranny.

I find myself agreeing with the late great George Carlin when he said: "They want obedient workers...they want people who are just smart enough to run the machines and do the paperwork."

Ouch! If that doesn't make you want to run out and take control of your life right now, I don't know what will. Remember, once you've harnessed your willpower, the best way to take control of your destiny is to learn how to manage money.

Money Management Resources

For detailed methods of money management, I recommend reading "The Complete Guide to Money" by Dave Ramsey, "The Barefoot Investor" by Scott Pape, and "I Will Teach You to Be Rich" by Ramit Sethi.

For developing a money-making mindset, I suggest reading "Think and Grow Rich" by Napoleon Hill, "The Richest Man in Babylon" by George Samuel Clason, and "Rich Dad, Poor Dad" by Robert Kiyosaki.

Freedom Points

I am not saying that you should make money the central concern of your life. Nor do I recommend a materialistic lifestyle. Rather I acknowledge that money plays a central role in our lives and in the lives of our loved ones. In the same way, that self-control and good habits are foundational, having control over your money is a foundational first step toward achieving financial freedom. It's true that a certain sacrifice of time and energy is required. But the peace of mind that comes from achieving financial stability repays the invested effort a thousand times over.

I call money "freedom points" because money gives you the freedom to maneuver in life. Are you trapped in a job that is slowly chipping away at your soul? Having money will give you the freedom to leave it. Is someone you love in need of a medical procedure they can't afford? Money will give you the freedom to help them.

Money is much more than a means of providing creature comforts. It is freedom itself. Is there a cost in terms of time and energy to become financially savvy? Absolutely. But being concerned about money doesn't mean you need to let it consume you. You can find the right balance between mastering your finances and tending to other equally important areas in your life.

The long story short is that if you don't want to be a drone under someone else's control, you have to do more than just earn a living. You also have to master your finances.

Breaking Free
If you are willing to have faith and take the leap forward – the rest of your life could be on the brink of changing. If there is anything I have learned from this whole experience, it is that you are the instrument of your own success,

Bear in mind that going back to full-time work isn't something to be ashamed of. In this life sometimes, we have to sacrifice our own happiness for the benefit of feeding those we hold dear, and there's not a thing wrong with that. I just hope there are others out there willing to break free because it has been one of the most rewarding things I have ever done.

Final Thoughts

I would recommend and actively encourage others to follow in my footsteps. The problem is: going with the flow is easy, it's simple, it's what we have been conditioned to do... and if you are not careful you will be trapped in it until the day you die.

The thing is – we only have one life, and it's ours. It doesn't belong to the manager, it doesn't belong to the company, and it certainly doesn't belong to the guy at the top, driving the Ferrari. It's yours. And what you choose to do with it matters. So, if you decide to work from 9 to 5 in a job you hate for the rest of your life – then that's on you. You don't like it? Go out and change it. Be the person you dreamed you'd be when you were a kid.

I mean that. If five-year-old you wanted to be an astronaut then you need to have a good, long and in-depth discussion with yourself about why you are working in a call center. What happened to that kid with the big dreams? Are they still in there? What would they say if they saw you leaving your own kids every day to go do something you hated?

Like I have said before – a good parent will do whatever it takes to make sure their family is clothed, housed and fed – and that is a perfectly valid priority. All I am suggesting is that you never give up on that kid. If you need to be in the 9 to 5 world for now, then be there. Just remember that you are patiently buying your time until you can get out of there and give that kid what it wants – a chance to be happy just being alive.

Make your plans – and never stop making your plans. Once you achieve one goal make yourself another. You can do or be anything you want to if you just take it one step at a time.

On a personal level, I believe one hundred percent that doing this, that taking this break, saved my life. I treasure each moment now, I love spending time with my family – and I'm a better person for them. If I had gone on the way I was, I don't think I would have lived to see retirement. The combination of pressure and stress would have broken me in the end. And that is the reason for this manuscript.

I hope that by reading this book and following some of the pointers of those who have gone before; you might be able to take firm hold of your own life, shake it by the neck and wring every last moment from it that you can. Maybe it doesn't mean leaving the 9 to 5 at all – maybe it just means making goals for yourself. Even if the only thing that you take away from this is that you might try meditation one day – that's enough for me.

After all, baby steps might be little, but they still get you there in the end.

www.ingramcontent.com/pod-product-compliance
Lightning Source LLC
Chambersburg PA
CBHW020605220526
45463CB00006B/2455